NEFERTITI

Lady of Grace

THE HISTORY HOUR

CONTENTS

INTRODUCTION

❦

There would be very few people in this world that would not recognize the regal bust of Nefertiti. It is enigmatic, iconic, and immensely beautiful. So beautiful in fact that Nefertiti has become the very epitome of beauty itself. Not only does she appear on every carrier bag in Cairo airport, but she is also pictured front and central on many beauty products.

❦

Ludwig Borchardt first recognized the potential of the Nefertiti bust in 1912 when he discovered it in an Amarna archaeological dig and partially hid it from the Egyptians view. He knew that he had found something special and presented photos not taken in the best light making it appear mundane. This led to his being able to remove the bust to Germany where it has been ever since.

It was not, however, completely, the beauty of the Nefertiti bust that caused Ludwig Borchardt to hide its attraction from the Egyptian authorities whom he brokered a deal with dividing the artifacts found. Rather it was the historical significance of owning a bust that depicted one of Egypt's most mysterious and reputedly powerful queens!

❧ II ❧
THE RISE OF NEFERTITI

"I wonder if our names determine our destiny, or if destiny leads us to choose certain names."
— **Michelle Moran, Nefertiti**

❦

Ludwig Borchardt was correct in his assumption that he had found an artifact of huge historical significance. Nefertiti has, since the busts discovery gone on to be one of the most sought after and discussed queens of the ancient Egyptian dynasties. Unfortunately, however, she has also proved to be one of the most elusive figures that to this very day frustratingly few facts are known about.

A BEAUTIFUL WOMAN HAS COME

❧

Prior to her marriage to Amenhotep IV, there is no factually proven historical record of Nefertiti at all. It is as though her life began, and as we will find out later, ended along with her husband's reign as Pharaoh. This is not, however, surprising considering that most evidence of her existence, along with Amenhotep IV, was mostly destroyed by later rulers of Egypt. Egyptians also did not record life, death, and everything in between in the manner that we do.

❧

It would have been unusual for Amenhotep IV to record any status that Nefertiti held on her marriage to him if she was a non-royal. Invariably only the highest ranking women would have been recorded as a king's daughter, a king's wife, and finally a king's mother. This did not happen with Nefertiti, in fact, Amenhotep IV was completely silent on her origin.

There were also no claims laid by anyone to being Nefertiti's parents. This was not unusual in the case of male relatives, who did not at this time make direct acknowledgments of any links with the royal family through marriage. Women, however, were different and seemed free to make their links known.

No woman is recorded, none the less, to have made claims of being Nefertiti's mother. This, of course, could be due to the possibilities we just have not found Nefertiti's mothers tomb yet, that she died before Nefertiti married, or that Nefertiti was in fact born abroad?

EMERGENCE FROM WITHIN THE HAREM

✧

There are two widely speculated theories of where Nefertiti came from, with the first being that she emerged from within Amenhotep IV inherited harem. This is not an unfeasible train of thought as many wives who were taken by Pharaohs did indeed come from this long-established source. To understand how this is a possibility, however, we need to understand the true nature of the harem.

✧

For many centuries the harem was viewed as a place where women lounged around on luxurious pillows in scanty clothing, and just waited to partake in sexual debauchery. Historians, however, have been able to debunk this myth revealing a whole different picture for the harems of ancient Egypt.

✧

In actual fact, the harems of Egypt would be better described as plain and simple women's quarters. They were no more or no less than a place where the women lived. Here they enjoyed a liberal society, but one that could be considered tedious. Day-to-day activities were seen as being beneath the harems remit, and the childcare that they were allowed to participate in was mainly handled by midwives.

❦

The women in the Egyptian harem included wives, queens, and princesses who were sent as gifts to the king. Marriages and relationships were often of a diplomatic nature in ancient Egypt rather than a matter of love. Tuthmose IV, Amenhotep IV grandfather, for example, married a princess of Mitanni. This was done to ensure the bitter rivalry that had been between the two kingdoms remained relatively stable.

❦

Multiple marriages were also not uncommon in ancient Egypt. Amenhotep IV father, Amenhotep III married at least six foreign princesses and multiple Egyptian women too. It would, in fact, be one of these very foreign princesses that would come to be the source of speculation for Nefertiti indeed emerging from the harem.

❦

Princess Tadukhepa was sent to Egypt to marry an ailing Amenhotep III by her father Tushratta of Mitanni, Syria. By the time she arrived, however, Amenhotep III was on his deathbed, and it is very unlikely the marriage was ever consummated.

❦

Following her new husband's death, Tadukhepa stayed within the harem and was handed down to Amenhotep IV who soon married her. Promptly after this Tadukhepa disappeared from public view never to emerge again. This and a number of other factors has led to the theory that Nefertiti was in actuality Tadukhepa renamed.

❦

Though the marriage date of Nefertiti was not recorded, it is believed by monumental evidence to have been just before or just after Amenhotep IV ascension. This would tie in with the theory of Nefertiti being Tadukhepa as they appear to have both married the king within a short period of his father dying.

❦

Regarding the name change from Tadukhepa to Nefertiti, supporters of this theory believe it was done to give the new queen of Egypt a less outlandish foreign name. They also believe that the meaning of Nefertiti, 'a beautiful woman has come,' supports the theory that she did indeed come from a foreign land.

❦

Furthermore, we also know that both women were relatively young since Tadukhepa is recorded as so, and Nefertiti went on to bear at least six children. Add all this to the fact that Tadukhepa disappeared as fast as she appeared and you appear to have a relatively good theory.

THE FIRST THEORY COLLAPSES

There is no doubting that the portrayal of Nefertiti as an exotic foreign princess is a pleasing one that comes with a certain romantic appeal. However, it is not one that is supported by actual archaeological or historical fact. Whilst it is certainly true that Tadukhepa married Amenhotep IV and promptly disappeared, it does not mean that she was indeed Nefertiti.

Throughout Amenhotep IV rule as Pharaoh of Egypt, it is known that he took several wives. Very few of these, with the exception of Nefertiti, however, are mentioned again within historical documents or findings. This would lead us to conclude that the disappearance of a wife from public view in ancient Egypt was simply a regular occurrence and not something to ponder on.

The assumed close dates of both the marriage to Nefertiti and Tadukhepa can also be easily explained away. Perhaps the marriages were not as close in date as people may believe, or it was a custom for multiple marriages to take place early in a new Pharaoh's reign.

To add another point of view Tushratta, Tadukhepa's father had also made it no secret that he wished for his daughter to be the queen of Egypt. In fact, in original negotiations with Amenhotep IV father, Amenhotep III, he had dictated that she should take the title of '*mistress of Egypt*.' No doubt these terms were accepted by Amenhotep III for peace-keeping reasons and may have been extended to his son, Amenhotep IV, and accepted.

Finally, in regard to the suggested name change to Nefertiti from an '*outlandish foreign one*,' there is precedence, even though it occurred later on in history, in the 19th dynasty. A Hittite Princess who was presented as a peace offering to Ramesses II was renamed Maathorneferure and made the great kings wife. However, since the emphasis for this theory is more on the meaning of the name Nefertiti than the name change itself, the precedence becomes irrelevant.

Records also show that all the Egyptian personal names given, except for the shortest, had a meaning. This meaning was usually either a reflection of the parent's devotion to a deity or characteristics of their child. Amenhotep, for example, means '*Amen is satisfied*,' whilst Neferneferure means '*exquisite beauty of Re*.' Since these names were given by the mother, it is not hard to imagine a proud one bestowing upon her child a name such as Nefertiti meaning '*a beautiful woman has come*.'

A MEMBER OF THE ROYAL
ELITE?

꧁꧂

The use of a question mark at the end of the heading in this section really has no need to be there as the evidence available now is enough to confirm that Nefertiti did, in fact, come from the royal elite. However, nothing is ever certain with the life of Nefertiti, and therefore the question mark remains as a shadow of that doubt.

꧁꧂

In an uncompleted tomb in the city of Amarna, the Lady Tey is depicted alongside her husband Ay receiving gold necklaces from the king and queen. This gifting at the time would have been seen as a great public honor reserved for high-ranking male officials and statesmen alone.

꧁꧂

The fact that a wife was receiving gold alongside her husband is a clear indication of how highly regarded Tey must have been. This is backed up by the fact that she was allowed to share an elaborate private tomb with her husband Ay on a more or less equal basis, and the titles she was given. These included *'nurse of the king's great wife, Nefertiti!'*

***

When used in the context it has been *'nurse'* would usually be translated to a wet nurse. This would appear to be backed up by a piece of a relief that was found in Amarna and is now kept in the Louvre museum. It shows an older woman wearing a distinctive gold necklace seated with a younger female on her knee. The older ladies breast is exposed, and she is presumed to be offering it to the younger charge.

***

Since Tey is the only woman that has been recognized as receiving gold as a reward from the king it is assumed that the older lady is her. The younger charge is thought to be Nefertiti and proof of the intimate relationship between her and Tey. It, however, is by no means certain as the relief has been badly damaged making definite identification impossible.

***

It was first supposed that Nefertiti being breastfed by a woman married to a man of high rank meant that she could have been born a royal princess. However, the fact that she never referred to herself as *'king's daughters'* as she would have done makes that speculation fruitless. Nefertiti was not a royal baby.

❧

The most likely explanation for Nefertiti being part of the royal elite actually exists in the relationship between herself and Tey's husband Ay. Ay was a court official prominently placed and holding the titles *'overseer of the king's horses'* and *'God's father.'* The latter would become Ay's favorite title with him being known universally as *'God's father Ay.'* Assuming this is not a priestly title and can be taken literally it would mean that Ay was Nefertiti's father.

❧

How this link between Nefertiti and Ay is made lies in the titles he was given and their meaning. Yuya, assumed to be Ay's father held both of the aforementioned titles before Ay. *'God's father'* was in reference to Yuya being father-in-law to Amenhotep III and father to his queen Tiy. Hence Ay being known as *'God's father'* too would presumably refer to Ay as Amenhotep IV father-in-law and his queen Nefertiti's father.

❧

Ay, however, makes no reference to himself being the father of Nefertiti but this is not surprising. As we have seen previously, it was not the domain of the males at the time to advertise their royal connections. Tey, his wife, on the other hand, does claim a link to the great Egyptian queen even though it is only as a wet nurse, and not as *'royal mother of the king's great wife.'*

❧

The fact that Tey does not claim Nefertiti as her daughter

would conclude that she was, in fact, her stepmother. After all, previous mothers of the Pharaoh's wives had all boasted of the fact. Thuyu, wife of Yuya, and Ay's mother is proof of this taking great delight in displaying her royal connection. This theory of a stepmother, however, leads us to a problem!

If Tey was indeed a stepmother to Nefertiti that would imply Ay had a first wife who had died. This, alone was not an uncommon occurrence as such tragedies happened in ancient Egypt just as they do today. However, there is no mention in Tey and Ay's tomb of a first wife, and the idea that Tey was breastfeeding Nefertiti poses problems of its own.

Is it conceivable that Ay simply married his wet nurse? Or are we taking the term wet nurse too literally? Could it have been by Egyptian linguistics standards wet nurse simply meant stepmother? Whatever the answer to these questions it is clear to see that the marriage of Nefertiti and Amenhotep IV raised Tey and Ay to a position of great honor within the court. For many a historian, this is the icing on the cake for the theory of Ay as Nefertiti's father.

A SISTER WHO SHEDS NO LIGHT

W hilst we can say nothing definite of Nefertiti's parentage we can be sure that she had a younger sister named Mutnodjmet. We know this as she was identified so in depictions of her with Neferti-ti's children and at other Amarna celebrations.

What we don't know, however, is whether Mutnodjmet was a full sister, half-sister, or even stepsister to Nefertiti. The term sister was used loosely at this time and could have meant any of the aforementioned. There is also no record of Mutnod-jmet's parentage, so this cannot help us either. What is clear is that she never claims to be of royal heritage just like Nefertiti.

Mutnodjmet disappears from all depictions and records just before Nefertiti's fourth child is born. The assumption from this is that she left the royal family, possibly to be married. She does not reappear.

❊ III ❊
THE MARRIAGE OF NEFERTITI

"You can't change the desert. You can only take the fastest course through it. Wishing it's an oasis won't make it so..."
— Michelle Moran, Nefertiti

❊

Wherever Nefertiti came from and whoever her parents were she would go on to make a marriage that would see her reign over Egypt with her husband for the next decade and more. It would not, however, be the traditional marriage that had been seen in Egypt before. Amenhotep IV and Nefertiti would certainly shake things up.

THE KING THAT MARRIED
NEFERTITI

❧

Amenhotep IV took over the rule of Egypt sometime in the mid-14th century BC from his father Amenhotep III. An exact date is unknown since reigns were not recorded by year but rather by the year of their reign. Historians have since been unable to pinpoint it any closer than the mid-14th century due to the removal of all records by future Pharaohs of Amenhotep IV reign and that of the two kings that followed him.

❧

We know, like Nefertiti, very little about Amenhotep IV before he came to the throne of Egypt. This is probably because from birth he was only second in line and therefore his elder brother Tuthmosis was the one seen in public life. There was no role for second born sons in ancient Egypt who were highly unlikely to ever take the throne. Amenhotep IV probably spent his younger years merely as an understudy for his older brother in case he was required to step in.

❀

Tuthmosis, the eldest son of Amenhotep III, by comparison to Amenhotep IV, was seen regularly in public life and would have undergone extensive training to fulfill his future role as king. This would, however, turn out be all in vain as Tuthmosis died at an early age leaving Amenhotep IV as his father's successor. This was a role he was clearly unprepared for and may account for his unusual reign.

❀

Like his father before him, Amenhotep IV chose to marry outside of the royal family itself. Prior to Amenhotep III reign most '*first wives*' were either sisters or half-sisters of the new pharaoh. Why this was the case, and both men chose to ignore tradition is unclear. What is clear, however, is that both men held their wives higher in status than previous other pharaohs perhaps had done.

FOR LOVE, POSITION OR LOOKS?

☙❦❧

Though we cannot ascertain why Amenhotep IV chose Nefertiti as his bride, we can deduce that the marriage was to all intents and purposes a happy one. There are many depictions of Nefertiti and Amenhotep IV together enjoying quality time with their children. This is perhaps not altogether surprising, as marriages in ancient Egypt, though arranged mainly for advancement purposes or political reasons, were still hoped to be ones that would blossom into love.

☙❦❧

It is therefore not inconceivable that Amenhotep IV chose Nefertiti because he was enamored of her or in love. Perhaps he had fallen for the great beauty that we now associate her with. However, the truth is regarding Nefertiti's looks, and we really are not sure how beautiful they were!

❦

As we are fairly confident that Nefertiti was of Egyptian descent, we can safely presume that she was light brown in skin color and had brown or black hair. Depictions from shortly after her marriage also show her as slightly shorter than her husband and of slender build. These portraits, however, cannot be taken literally as the art during the 18th dynasty was created with more artistic license than reality.

❦

Since we know nothing concrete of Nefertiti's upbringing or parentage we cannot know for certain or even speculate if the marriage was made for political reasons. A higher position, however, can be ascertained as Nefertiti clearly rose from the royal elite to actual royalty.

FAMILY AND STATUS

❧

I t is clear from the poetry written by Amenhotep IV himself that if he didn't love Nefertiti on their marriage that he certainly fell in love with her during. He wrote

'And the heiress, Great in the palace, Fair of face,
Adorned with the double plumes, Mistress of
happiness, Endowed with favours, At hearing
whose voice the king rejoices, The Chief wife of
the King, His beloved, The lady of the two lands,
Neferneferuaten - Nefertiti, May she live forever
and always.'

❧

When Amenhotep IV makes mention of 'the chief wife of
the king' he is referring to Nefertiti as the highest in status of
his wives. Like many pharaohs before him and many after he

did also marry other women. Tadukhepa whom we know disappeared shortly after marrying Amenhotep IV was just one. The king also married, to our knowledge, Kiya, Meritaten, and Ankhesenamun.

❧

Nefertiti, in regard to the additional marriages, would probably have thought little of them. Pharaohs throughout all the dynasty's preceding and forthcoming took more than one wife as, if nothing more, a matter of tradition.

❧

During their reign together Nefertiti and Amenhotep IV had six children together, all girls. They were, Ankhesenamaten, Meritaten, Meketaten, Neferneferuaten - the - younger, Neferneferune, and Setepenre. Ankhesenamun and Meritaten would go on to marry future pharaohs Tutankhamen and Smenkhkare, but not before they married their father!

OTHER WIVES

W e have very little record of Amenhotep IV additional wives, other than Tadukhepa, Kiya, Meritaten, and Ankhesenamun. These four are mentioned in writings and one, Kiya, is shown in depictions of the king with Nefertiti missing. She does not, however, appear for very long before Nefertiti re-emerges and takes back over from her in the historical records.

Why there was a period of time when Nefertiti disappears and another queen appears by the king's side is a mystery, but it is possible and feasible, that it was during a time when the king was trying to achieve a male heir to take over from him after he died. What is certain, however, is that although Kiya appears to be of import to Amenhotep IV, she would never be, and nor would any woman ever be, of as high importance to the king as Nefertiti.

❧

Tadukhepa, assuming that she indeed was not Nefertiti, seems to be the first and least important of the wives that Amenhotep IV took. In fact, it is highly probable, as stated previously, that she was just part of some political dealings. No records exist for her after the marriage took place.

❧

Meritaten was Amenhotep IV second born daughter who would later go on to marry the future king Smenkhkare. Smenkhkare is in turn believed to be Meritatens half-sister on her father's side. Why Amenhotep IV married his daughter goes unrecorded, but it could have been purely to raise her social status.

❧

This, however, is not necessarily the case as ancient Egyptians often married close relatives such as brothers and sisters and had incestuous relationships. Brother and sister marriages are understood to have taken place to keep the bloodline of the succession pure.

❧

Ankhesenamun was Amenhotep IV eldest daughter born as Ankhesenamaten. She would later go on to marry Tutankhamen who in turn was her half-brother on her father's side. Her name was changed three years into Tutankhamen's rule to erase to her father's cult of Aten. Again there is no record of why Amenhotep IV married another of his daughters.

Kiya is the only other recorded wife of Amenhotep IV that appears to have come anywhere near the status which he bestowed on Nefertiti. Little, however, is known about her. Even her name has been cause for debate with some historians believing that it is a Mitanni princess title and others that it is native Egyptian.

What we do know about Kiya is that she was bestowed such titles as '*the favorite*' and '*the greatly beloved*' in regard to the king. Her full title recorded on inscriptions was

> 'the wife and greatly beloved of the king of upper and lower Egypt, living in truth, lord of the two lands, Neferkheperure Waenre, the goodly child of the living Aten, who shall be living for ever and ever, Kiya.'

Clearly, Kiya was an important wife to Amenhotep IV but she strangely only appears on artifacts that derive from Amarna. This would lead us to conclude that she was not Amenhotep IV wife before this period. Some historians have suggested that Kiya was the mother to future pharaohs Tutankhamen and Smenkhkare which would explain her importance. She had provided him with the male heirs he so desperately needed.

Kiya disappears from the historical record during the last period of Amenhotep IV reign. One of the last documented records of her name is on a wine docket that refers to it being Amenhotep IV eleventh year of reign. It is not known whether she died, was banished, or suffered some unknown fate. Some historians suggest banished is the most likely circumstance as her name had been replaced on inscriptions which those of Amenhotep IV eldest daughter Meritaten.

❧ IV ☙
THE CULT OF ATEN

"Nothing is forever...nothing lasts."
— **Michelle Moran, Nefertiti**

❧❧❧

To the reader of this, it must seem incredible that we have come so far into this world-renowned woman's life with so little fact and so much conjecture? We are left with absolutely no concept, at this point, of who Nefertiti was or how she would play her role as queen of Egypt.

NEFERTITI AND AMENHOTEP IV
EARLY RULE

Like any other queen of Egypt, Nefertiti's story can only be told through the story of her husband. The couple is intrinsically linked with Amenhotep IV fundamentally controlling Nefertiti's life. It is for this reason that any biography of Nefertiti must also be the biography of Amenhotep IV and vice versa.

During years one to five of his reign Amenhotep IV continued mainly in his father's footsteps. His court remained at Thebes, more than likely based at the Malkata Palace, and he continued building work his father had begun. It is during this time too that Nefertiti makes her first appearance in the damaged tomb of the royal butler Pareneffer.

Accompanied by her royal husband Nefertiti is shown worshipping the sun god Aten. A telling sign of things to come as Amenhotep IV would go on to order a temple built dedicated to Aten the sun god shortly after. This was the first step in what would soon become a religious revolution that Nefertiti would albeit at her husband's side play a large part in.

৺৵৺

The temple Akhenaten IV built was named the Gempaaten meaning '*the Aten is found in the estate of the Aten*.' It consisted of a series of buildings which included a structure named the Hwt Benben that Amenhotep IV dedicated to his wife, Nefertiti. This was not the only Aten temple built at this time as Amenhotep IV also constructed the Rud-menus and the Teni-menu at Karnak too.

RELIGIOUS WORSHIP IN
ANCIENT EGYPT

☙❧

Ancient Egyptian religion centered on the worship of deities that they believed were around them and in control of their world. For the royal family, this meant worshipping Gods such as Amen, Horus, and Bastet. Egyptians believed it was incredibly important to please their Gods and Goddesses in order to be given their favor.

☙❧

Pharaohs were relied on immensely to obtain the favor of the Gods as it was believed that they possessed divine powers by the gift of their position. They were the intermediaries between the Gods and the people and therefore responsible for keeping them happy. They did this by providing offerings and performing rituals. A huge amount of resources went into funding these practices including the building of immense and ornate temples.

During the first four years of Amenhotep IV reign, although his religious leanings were going in the direction of worshipping just one god, the Aten, he did not repress the traditional worship of Amen. In fact, the priest of Amen was certainly still in place at this time.

THE RISE OF ATEN AND AMARNA

It is not clear why Amenhotep IV decided to eradicate all Gods other than Aten, but he certainly went about it wholeheartedly. He simply demanded and received a ruthless rejection of them all. He also had a new capital city constructed away from Thebes which was entirely dedicated to the worship of Aten. Or so he may have believed!

Amarna, or Akhetaten as it was formerly known, was built on the East bank of the river Nile some 250 miles north of Thebes. Building began, it is estimated, either sometime in the fourth year of Amenhotep IV rule or the fifth. To ensure it was completed quickly buildings were constructed from mud brick and whitewashed with more important structures being stone-faced. It was finally finished in Amenhotep IV ninth year of rule although he did not wait that long to move himself and his family there. Nefertiti, Akhenaten, and their children took up residence in year five.

Once in residence in Amarna, Amenhotep IV is believed to have tried to create a monotheism and partially succeeded. Some of his court changed their names to remove their patronage to other Gods and deities and place them under Aten. Others, however, such as Thutmose *'child of Thoth'*, who carved the Nefertiti bust did not, and evidence has since been found that even in Amarna, the center of *'Aten's cult,'* other deities continued to be worshipped.

On arriving at Amarna Amenhotep IV also took a new name, Akhenaten, to honor the deity that he worshipped. He renamed Nefertiti too, Neferneferuaten - Nefertiti meaning *'beautiful are the beauties of Aten, a beautiful woman has come*.' This and the subsequent role she seems to have played in the reign of Amenhotep IV (Akhenaten) is why we now believe her to have been so powerful.

LIFE IN AMARNA AND AT THE ROYAL COURT

There is no reason to believe that life in Amarna was any different to that of life in Thebes, except for the religious worship of Aten. Plans have been found for the city of Amarna which show great detail of the layout including the royal families residence, administerial and ceremonial buildings, and houses of the cities nobles. Away from the city is Akhenaten's royal necropolis, east of the city and built within the cliffs.

What life would have been like here for Nefertiti is unclear as only documented evidence of kings daily rituals have been discovered. Amenhotep IV would have most likely spent his days hunting, meeting with his advisors and attending lavish parties that the royal elite was known to take great pleasure in.

⚜

No doubt Nefertiti also attended these parties with their music, plentiful food, and revelry. However, what she did with her days is mainly unknown. We can state that she spent some of her time with her husband and family through depictions found showing scenes of this. We can also assume from other depictions she spent lots of time in worship. We cannot, however, state with any certainty that she attended Amenhotep IV meetings with his advisors.

NEFERTITI'S ROLE IN THE CULT
OF ATEN

❧

Even before leaving Thebes for Amarna it is immensely clear that Amenhotep IV, who we shall now refer to as his new name Akhenaten, held Nefertiti in high regard, and that she was given a ranking few other queens had enjoyed. Depictions have been found of her acting in previously '*king only*' roles offering gifts, worshipping Gods, and driving chariots. Proof that at some point in her early reign with Akhenaten Nefertiti had abandoned the role of a passive observer of his reign and become more active.

❧

Further proof also lies in the discovery of a group of blocks which depict Nefertiti smiting a female enemy on a royal boat. She is wearing her trademark blue headdress, is naked from the waist up, and poised to strike the blow with a mace or sword. The very fact that smiting was a king's duty again shows us that Nefertiti had indeed risen in both ritualistic and political importance.

※※※

Once in Amarna Nefertiti's apparent power did not wane, in fact, it grew. During her time in Amarna, she became probably the most depicted queen in Egyptian history with arguably more than twice the amount of appearances on later found reliefs and blocks than Akhenaten himself.

※※※

The temple of Gempaaten, especially the Hwt Ben Ben built for Nefertiti by Akhenaten is a particularly good example of how important she had become. It displayed an amazing array of depictions, columns, and statues dedicated to Nefertiti. Unfortunately, most of these were destroyed by Haremheb when he wiped Nefertiti and Akhenaten from existence, but they have since been re-discovered. They had been used as inner stonework in later buildings by the future pharaoh Haremheb.

※※※

Examples of these frequent depictions can be seen in the four pillars that would have made up a colonnade. On three sides they have been decorated with almost full-length depictions of Nefertiti and her daughter Meritaten. They are shaking their sistra's in the worship of Aten.

※※※

On the fourth side of the pillars, presumed to be the '*special* side' that would have faced the courtyard, there is a four-part depiction of a scene in which Nefertiti makes offerings to Aten. Behind her, Meritaten also appears, a perfect miniature replica of her mother. Above both mother and daughter, the sun's disc is seen with the sun's rays reaching down to accept their offerings.

Interestingly, the stance of the queen in these depictions is that of a king making offerings to the Gods. Within the temple, the same story is told with Nefertiti and one or two of her daughters being shown making offerings to the Gods. There is no sign of Akhenaten in any of these depictions. In fact, no other human nor animal appear anywhere here.

HENRI CHEVRIER'S NEFERTITI
BLOCKS

As we know, Hwt Benben was mostly taken apart by King Haremheb who mainly used the blocks in future buildings. These blocks, however, were not used in a haphazard or unthoughtful manner as Henri Chevrier discovered in the 1940s. The Nefertiti blocks rather had been carefully reconstructed into at least partial scenes.

Curiously, at least two of the recovered scenes had been reconstructed upside down, presumably purposefully. Damage had also been done to many of the images of Nefertiti, and her fingers had been slashed where they met with the rays of the Aten. This seems an odd act considering care had been taken to reassemble the scenes correctly.

Historians have only been able to come to the conclusion that the damage was an act of disrespect and revenge against a queen whose husband had been labeled a heretic. They had turned her upside down, slashed her image and hidden her from view behind thick stone walls.

BACK TO NEFERTITI'S ROLE IN
THE CULT OF ATEN

❧

Why Nefertiti rose to the apparent status that she did whilst in Amarna could be credited to two factors. One, Akhenaten allowed her to reign as his co-regent or close to, or two she was transformed into a Goddess. The latter would seem to be more feasible due to a problem Akhenaten was faced with concerning his new religion.

❧

In traditional Egyptian religion motherly Goddesses that represented fertility were of high importance. Akhenaten had, however, removed all trace of these Goddesses when he installed his new religion. Aten was, in essence, a male God and had no female counterpart. Akhenaten needed to implement a female aspect to Aten and who better to promote than the strong wife he had already made powerful?

❦

This was not as huge a leap as it may seem as many queens had served as priestesses and were thought to have semi-divine origins the same as the king. Akhenaten could easily make Nefertiti his female counterpart, the complement to his male role. Akhenaten, Aten, and Nefertiti would form a semi-divine triad.

❦

With her new role, Nefertiti was elevated in position within depictions of the royal family. Instead of standing slightly behind or next to the king, she was now shown as facing him. This provided a pleasing symmetrical view of king facing queen with the Aten in the sky centrally above them.

❦

Nefertiti's power, however, is not only shown in her appearance by his side, or facing him at events and times that would historically have only involved the king, but also by her attire. During her early reign, she adopted a Nubian style close-cropped wig which had only been previously worn by soldiers who fought in the Pharaoh's army. This style wig would henceforth be associated with those closest to the king.

❦

Nefertiti's style of headdress also changed as she became more powerful. At the start of her reign, she wears a traditional queens headdress like her predecessors. Eventually, however, this changes and she begins to wear her own unique style. It is tall, straight-edged and very reminiscent of the one that she wears in her famous bust. Though the origins of this style of headdress are unknown, it is believed that it is a feminine version of a king's crown.

※

With the evidence, historians have found it would be difficult to argue that Nefertiti was not one of the most powerful queens in Egyptian history. It is, however, difficult to decipher in what capacity. Did she rule as a co-regent alongside her husband Akhenaten, or was she simply a much needed Goddess for his new religious cult?

NEFERTITI - CO-REGENT OR GODDESS?

꧁꧂

O n a private depiction of Nefertiti and Akhenaten enjoying time with their children lies a long-debated image of the possibility of co-regency. Akhenaten is seated upon a simple stool that is undecorated holding his eldest daughter in his arms. Nefertiti, by compari-son, is seated upon a slightly lower stool but one that is more adorned with decoration and appears more regal. She too has one of their children seated on her knee.

꧁꧂

Whilst this depiction of the family is not unusual, the seating arrangement is! Why is Nefertiti seated upon an obviously regal motiffed stool whilst her husband occupies a plain one? Could it be that she was indeed Akhenaten's co-regent and that this family portrait was intended to show her power? Or was it just a simple mistake by the depictions artist?

༺✿༻

It would, of course, be very easy to simply ask why, if Nefertiti had been Akhenaten's co-regent, he didn't just proclaim it? Perhaps he did, and we just haven't found it yet. However, with an absolute lack of evidence to support this theory we cannot just assume it. The argument for Nefertiti as co-regent of Egypt at this time has to rely on supposition and deductions made from the existing evidence. This is simply not enough to be definitive proof.

༺✿༻

So was Nefertiti a Goddess? Well, she was certainly promoted to a far more important role with the installation of the cult of Aten. She becomes the semi-divine female figure of the Aten triad. However, this does not mean that she was raised to divine status as a Goddess, she could have simply been a priestess.

༺✿༻

The argument for the idea of Nefertiti as a Goddess is backed up by the discovery of Akhenaten's sarcophagus in the royal Amarna tomb. On it, the four corners have been decorated with raised reliefs of Nefertiti. She has been created to appear as though she is embracing and protecting the king. Whilst these figures are clumsy and do not particularly resemble Nefertiti we can be sure that it is indeed her as they have been quite clearly labeled.

༺✿༻

The belief that this makes Nefertiti a Goddess lies within the fact that future kings also chose to embellish their sarcophagi with images of women. Goddesses such as Isis, Neith, and Selket were chosen. But does this automatically mean that Nefertiti herself was a Goddess, or could it mean something else? Perhaps Akhenaten simply liked the idea of a woman protecting his body after death, and as all other Goddesses were now unavailable to him, he chose his beloved wife.

One way we could be a little more certain of Nefertiti as a Goddess is if future kings themselves used her on their sarcophagus. Unfortunately, however, we only have one possible sarcophagus that could prove it, and that is of Tutankhamen. His sarcophagus was discovered to have been clearly altered although it did still depict four goddesses. Sadly, none of these goddesses can be identified as Nefertiti meaning we have no proof of her as a definite Goddess.

❧ V ❧

THE DISAPPEARANCE OF NEFERTITI

"My love is unique an none can rival her. Just by passing, she has already stolen away my heart."
— Michelle Moran, Nefertiti

❧❧❧

In the twelfth year of Akhenaten's reign, Nefertiti suddenly disappears from view. She is last depicted in public as appearing at a huge celebration thrown by Akhenaten which ambassadors from Libya, Nubia and the Mediterranean islands attended. The king is also accompanied by his six daughters who all stand under the protection of sunshades from the hot Egyptian sun.

WHERE DID SHE GO?

❧

Shortly after the celebrations Meketaten, the third born daughter of Nefertiti and Akhenaten died as the result of a plague that was rampant at the time. It may be no coincidence that other members of the royal family also disappeared during this time too. Meketaten was laid to rest in her father's tomb, and it is here that we can see poignant illustrations of Nefertiti and Akhenaten grieving over their lost daughter.

❧

When historians first discovered that Nefertiti no longer appears from year twelve of Akhenaten's reign they believed a number of theories were possible. Had Nefertiti died of the rampant plague herself? Had she committed suicide at the grief over the loss of her daughter? Could she have, for some reason unknown, been banished from the court, or had she retired?

❦

As it turned out only one of these theories could have been remotely possible because historians later discovered that Nefertiti reemerges in Akhenaten's sixteenth year of reign. So where had she been for those four years that she is missing from public life, what had happened?

❦

The answer to this is nobody knows, but it is highly likely that nothing occurred and Nefertiti continued to be at her husband's side. The absence of any proof of this could simply be down to later destruction of depictions of Akhenaten and Nefertiti and nothing sinister at all.

❦

There is, of course also the possibility that Akhenaten favored another wife at this time, as he had done at least once before with Kiya. There is, however, no evidence of this as Kiya appeared in depictions of Akhenaten at the time she was in favor, and none have been discovered with another queen for the period Nefertiti was missing.

❦

Finally, there is also the one theory that could hold some weight. Nefertiti was banished from by her husband Akhenaten's side for some unknown crime we know nothing about. Speculation as to a possible reason for this has included Nefertiti's failure to provide Akhenaten with a male heir, that she questioned the validity of his new religion, or even that she turned her back on it completely. None of these, however, seem in the least bit feasible so Nefertiti's absence during this time will have to remain just another one of her mysteries.

RE-EMERGENCE IN YEAR SIXTEEN

❦

In 2012, concrete evidence was found that Nefertiti was indeed alive in the sixteenth year of Akhenaten's rule. A regnal year sixteen, month three inscription mentions the royal wife being present and says

'the great royal wife, his beloved, mistress of the two lands, Neferneferuaten - Nefertiti.'

❦

Little more after the inscription is dated is known about Nefertiti's life nor that of her husband. It is generally accepted, however, that Akhenaten himself died in the seventeenth year of his reign. Whether Nefertiti had died before him or lived on after him is unknown and remains a source of huge speculation.

❧ VI ❧
THE CONTINUATION OF NEFERTITI

"In Egypt, there is a saying: When good fortune looks down upon us, it does so in threes, one for each part of the Eye of Horus. His upper lid, his lower lid and the eye itself."
— **Michelle Moran, Nefertiti**

❧

For those who believe Nefertiti lived passed the death of her husband, there are many debated possibilities as to what happened next in her life. These include the possibility that Nefertiti herself ruled as Pharaoh, that she went on to be co-regent for the next Pharaohs, or that she just quietly retired.

ALL HAIL KING NEFERTITI

It is historically accepted that after Akhenaten's death the reign of Egypt passed to Neferneferuaten, Smenkhkare, and finally onto the infamous Tutankhamen. However, this is where the accepted theory ends, and the speculation begins.

As with Akhenaten and Nefertiti herself, there is very little documented information about the reigns of Neferneferuaten and Smenkhkare, or who they were. Smenkhkare is a particularly shaded character who appeared to spring from nowhere, rule for a short period, and then vanish into thin air. No relationship to the royal family has been found for him, no tomb exists, and there has been nobody recovered. Smenkhkare is little more than a carved name.

The belief that has sprung from these two shadowy kings of Egypt is that one or both could possibly be Nefertiti. That she as powerful as she had become beside her husband could have gone on to rule Egypt alone. This is rather an attractive theory as it clears up several mysteries with just one solution. Where did Nefertiti go? Well, she became king. Who were Neferneferuaten and Smenkhkare? They were both Nefertiti as king.

🐉

The argument for Nefertiti as Neferneferuaten cannot be proved or disproved. It is true that during her husband's reign Nefertiti was a strong and powerful figure, possibly even co-regent. This would make her succeeding Akhenaten to the throne of Egypt at least credible. Add the fact that Neferneferuaten is accepted to have been a woman, and the theory comes alive even more.

🐉

To back the theory of Nefertiti as Neferneferuaten even further there has been a document found in the ancient city of Hittite, capital of Hattusa, which dates back to the Amarna period and contains extraordinary content. This document is a letter from the queen of Egypt to the Hittite ruler and says

> 'My husband has died and I have no son. They say about you that you have many sons. You might give me one of your sons to become my husband. I would not wish to take one of my subjects as a husband...I am afraid.'

⬥

The identity of the queen who wrote this letter is not revealed by name but rather is called Dakhamunza, a translation of the Egyptian title Tahemetnesu, meaning '*kings wife*.' Possible candidates are Nefertiti, Meritaten, and Ankhesenamun with the latter originally being the favorite.

⬥

Ankhesenamun was the wife of Tutankhamen and daughter of Nefertiti and Akhenaten. Sadly, Tutankhamen died leaving no male heir and no obvious one to choose to follow him. This is why it was believed originally that Ankhesenamun was the most likely candidate as the author of the Hittite letter. However, this was based on the timing of reigns that were later discovered to be false making Ankhesenamun an unlikely author of the letter and Nefertiti more likely.

⬥

In regard to Nefertiti as being Smenkhkare, we can be a little more sure in ruling in or ruling out the possibility. On a very basic level, Smenkhkare is known to have married Nefertiti's daughter Meritaten making it seem impossible that Smenkhkare was Nefertiti. This is unless, as some theorists believe, Nefertiti disguised herself as a man to rule Egypt and married her daughter to elevate her status!

⬥

Whether Nefertiti could have disguised herself as a man in order to rule Egypt or not becomes rather irrelevant when you consider evidence that was clarified in 2000. In 1906-7 a tomb was discovered that held a body which on examination was believed to be Akhenaten. However, this identification did not hold up when it was found the bones were that of a man no older than twenty-five years of age.

❦

Further analysis, including the investigations done in 2000 concluded that in actual fact the body probably belonged to Smenkhkare. This was based on the craniofacial morphology very closely resembling that of Tutankhamen. Based on this it was concluded that the body had to be either Tutankhamen's father, brother, or son.

❦

Since we know that Akhenaten was Tutankhamen's father, and he was older than twenty-five when he died we can rule out the possibility that the body is that of his father. We can also rule out that it was his son as Tutankhamen was not old enough to have a twenty-year-old son at the time of his death. Depictions within the tomb show Tutankhamen as being alive when the body was interred.

❦

This only leaves the possibility that the body found was that of a brother of Tutankhamen. This would fit with the time-line of ascension if Smenkhkare was the older brother who died young passing the crown of Egypt to Tutankhamen. It also, more interestingly elevates the possibility of Nefertiti as Neferneferuaten. After all, it would make sense that the reign of Egypt was passed from Akhenaten to Nefertiti to his sons.

It would not, however, have made sense for it to pass from Akhenaten to an unknown female before his sons. Clearly, Smenkhkare judging by the fact he died around age twenty-five would have been old enough to take the crown on his father Akhenaten's death.

ALL HAIL CO-REGENT
NEFERTITI

Co-regency was certainly not unheard of in Egyptian times, in fact, it was fairly commonplace. Several future kings ruled alongside their fathers before taking the regency on their father's deaths. It was also not unheard of for the queen to rule alongside their children or their dead husbands if those children were too young to rule on their own.

The theory of Nefertiti as co-regent turns the timeline of ancient Egyptian kings on its head. It places Smenkhkare as reigning immediately after his father followed by Nefernefer-uaten and finally Tutankhamen. This perhaps makes more sense than the generally accepted timeline but why?

It would make more sense that Akhenaten passed the rule of Egypt directly to his son Smenkhkare rather than a woman who is very much an unknown or his wife. In fact, it is possible that Akhenaten was already grooming his son to take over before he died in the form of making him co-regent.

❧

If this is the case and Smenkhkare took over as pharaoh on his father's death Nefertiti would have faded into the background as Tiy, Akhenaten's mother had done before her. She would have been retired, as we know it in modern terms, and no longer part of or portrayed in depictions of royal life.

❧

When Smenkhkare died, and at an early age, the reign of Egypt would then have passed to his younger brother Tutankhamen. He, however, would only have been nine or ten years old and considered too young to rule on his own. He would have needed a co-regent or someone to rule as regent for him, and this is where Nefertiti comes in.

❧

As people in ancient Egypt commonly died young the tradition of a king not old enough to rule on their own having their mother rule with or for them was certainly not unheard of. That Nefertiti was only Tutankhamen's stepmother would have made no difference. She could have stepped up to rule alongside the new king, or more likely for him. The likelihood of ruling for him is made more feasible since Nefertiti, if the theory is correct, took her regnal name back, Neferneferuaten.

In the third year of Tutankhamen's reign, he began to reverse the religious changes that his father Akhenaten had made. He ended the worship of Aten and restored the God Amen. This was on the advice of his advisors suggesting that Nefertiti by this time was not ruling for him or alongside him. It would be very hard to believe that Nefertiti would have ended the worship of Aten herself considering how devoted she had been to him during her husband's reign.

FADING INTO OBSCURITY OR
RETURNING HOME

Whether or not Nefertiti went on to rule Egypt or be a co-regent would have had no effect on what eventually would happen to her. If her rule or co-rule ended, and she was still alive, she would have liked her mother-in-law before her faded into obscurity, essentially retiring.

This is not to say that Nefertiti would not have appeared in any depictions of the era, but it would have been rare, and the chances of finding them even rarer. Haremhab, a future pharaoh, destroyed much of the evidence that existed of Akhenaten to Tutankhamen's rule.

Though it has been pretty much ruled out by most historians, there are still those who believe Nefertiti could have hailed from a foreign country such as Syria. This has led them to offer the option that after her husband's death, co-regency, or rule, Nefertiti simply returned home.

❧ VII ❧

THE DEATH AND BURIAL
OF NEFERTITI

"Because he is weak and shallow, and you should learn to recognize men who are afraid of others with power, Mutnodjmet."
— **Michelle Moran, Nefertiti**

❧

Whilst it is uncertain what happened to Nefertiti on the death of her husband, or if she was even alive when he died, it is certain that at some point she did indeed pass away. It is also certain that most biographies of a person's life would end here, citing the date of death, the burial, and legacy. However, as with all things Nefertiti it was never going to be that simple!

BURIAL OF ROYALTY IN
ANCIENT EGYPT

❦

The ancient Egyptians practiced funeral rituals that would ascertain the journey of their soul into the afterlife. This afterlife, however, was not the ascent into heaven that we foresee as our destiny, but rather an eternal Egypt that mirrored the individual's life.

❦

By the 18th dynasty, the rituals of burial had become incredibly elaborate regarding royalty. Their burial chambers contained many riches that they would need to take with them into the afterlife, and the walls were painted with scenes depicting their everyday lives. Food, gold, practical items, even servants and pets were entombed with the body.

❦

The body itself also needed preparing for the afterlife and

were generally stripped of their organs which were stored in jars for treatment and return to the body later. The body itself was then rubbed down with salt to dry it out, then washed and stuffed with linen. Once organs had been replaced, the body was then wrapped in strips of linen with amulets and prayer cloths to protect them.

❧

Finally, the wrapped body was then placed in a sarcophagus which was ornately decorated, in general, to resemble the deceased. These sarcophagi were then placed in their burial tombs, after months of burial rites were completed, and left to start their eternal life.

❧

Due to the elaborate decoration and depictions within ancient Egyptian tombs, many mummies have been able to be identified on discovery. However, many have also suffered over time, being destroyed by the ravages of centuries untouched or foul play. Others have simply either not been discovered, or have been moved to tombs unrelated to them making them virtually impossible to identify.

WHAT DID NEFERTITI DIE OF
AND WHERE IS SHE BURIED?

❦

When Nefertiti disappeared in the twelfth year of Akhenaten's reign, it was believed that she had died of the plague. This, it would seem, would have been the most feasible explanation since her daughter Mekataten, Kiya, another of Akhenaten's wives, and other members of the royal family also succumbed to it. However, with the discovery of the inscription proving Nefertiti was alive in the sixteenth year this theory had to be relinquished.

❦

Since we have no further evidence of Nefertiti in life other than theories, which we cannot ascertain, we cannot even begin to look for her cause of death. We can, however, probably safely assume that it was before the reign of Haremhab approximately thirteen years later. This is not because Haremhab would necessarily have mentioned Nefertiti during his reign but rather because he tried to destroy all trace of her and Akhenaten. This could only have been presumably thought to be possible if the great lady herself had died.

Where Nefertiti is buried is yet to be established. It is just another piece of the jigsaw puzzle that is Nefertiti that remains to be solved. We can, however, speculate or offer theories based on Egyptian traditional burial sites and what little facts we have.

Traditionally royal couples would have shared a tomb that was built specifically for them. There is evidence that Akhenaten planned exactly this but at Amarna rather than in the Valley of the Kings. No evidence has been found, however, of that tomb being completed never mind being used for his own or Nefertiti's burial.

Akhenaten's sarcophagus has been located and identified and now stands in the Cairo museum. It was not found at Amarna, however, but rather at a tomb in the Valley of the Kings. Upon finding it, archeologists discovered that the sarcophagus had been destroyed to the point of needing reconstruction. The royal funerary mask with it had also suffered damage that is now stated as being deliberate. Did future king Haremhab find it at Amarna and try to destroy it along with everything else?

Locating Akhenaten's coffin but not Nefertiti's with it probably raises more questions than it answers. If Akhenaten and Nefertiti had been laid to rest together why was her sarcophagus not removed along with his and placed in the tomb at the Valley of the Kings? And if it wasn't, what happened to it? Had Haremhab possibly got his hands on it as well as Akhenaten's? If so had he destroyed it to the point it was immovable? If he had why has it not been found at Amarna?

The questions surrounding the death of Nefertiti are endless and will no doubt continue for many years to come. That is unless by some stroke of luck or genius Nefertiti's final resting place is uncovered. Several times over the years excitement has been incited over the possible discovery, but each time there has been deflation as the possibility has proved to be false.

THE YOUNGER LADY

I n 1898, French archeologist Victor Loret located two females mummies inside a tomb that contained Amenhotep II in the Valley of the Kings. These two mummies became known as the '*younger lady*' and the '*elderly lady*,' and it was announced in 2003 that Nefertiti was a likely candidate for being the younger of the two.

Joann Fletcher who led the team investigating the '*younger lady*' mummy claimed that mummification techniques used on the body were that of the 18th dynasty, that the age of the body was correct, and that the arm had been bent into a position reserved for pharaohs. Furthermore, she revealed, they had also found a rare wig akin to those worn by Nefertiti and embedded Nefer beads.

This theory of Nefertiti as the *'younger lady'* was received with varying degrees of enthusiasm. Critics stated that the only positive way to identify the mummy as Nefertiti was through DNA and that since no member of her family had been identified this would not be possible. They also went on to state that the wig and arm position were not proof enough alone. The wig had been merely discovered near the mummy not conclusively making it hers, and the arm position was not exclusive to a pharaoh's royal family. As for the 18th dynasty connection, there were over a hundred royal wives and daughters in that period that the mummy could be.

At the time the claim was made Egyptian archeologist Dr. Zaiha Hawass dismissed the claim of the *'younger lady'* as Nefertiti stating that there was insufficient evidence. Later that year he would go even further in his dismissal by claiming that the *'younger lady'* was, in fact, a male. More recently, however, CT scans have been performed on this mummy resulting in the finding that the mummy is not, in fact, male but female as first thought. It is not, however, the body of Nefertiti, rather it is more likely to be an unidentified daughter of Amenhotep III.

THE HIDDEN CHAMBER

A second possibility for the location of Nefertiti's body was discovered by British archeologist Nicholas Reeves in 2015. He had been studying scans of Tutankhamen's tomb when he discovered what he thought was a possible hidden doorway or structural anomaly with another chamber possibly behind it.

The reason behind Reeve's thinking that a chamber with Nefertiti in it was a possibility was the knowledge that Tutankhamen was known to have moved several sarcophagi during his reign. These 'moves' occurred during or after his third year of reign when he returned to the worship of Amen and the city of Thebes.

In March 2016, further research on the potentially hidden chamber was conducted. A ground penetrating radar scan was conducted and indeed revealed two empty spaces. These spaces had what appeared to be organic and metallic elements inside them. However, when the University of Turin stepped in and conducted their own sonar scan of the area, they claimed to find nothing. Based on this further excavation such as breaking through to the chambers has been refused.

A DISCOVERY IN LUXOR

✦

In early 2018 a tomb was discovered on the banks of the river Nile at El-Asasef, Luxor. This tomb was almost perfectly preserved and contained the sarcophagi of one rishi style 17th dynasty mummy and one, excitingly, 18th-century one.

✦

Though the excavation of this tomb was started in March, it paused in May and restarted in August. Along with the sarcophagi, many other mummies were discovered with dating pointing to the fact the tomb is over four thousand years old.

✦

Whilst there have been no claims yet as to who the 18th

dynasty sarcophagus may belong to, it was only opened very recently, we may yet see some made. Thebes, where Tutankhamen moved sarcophagi too, is located within the ancient city of Luxor making Nefertiti, although a remote one, at least a possibility.

IN PLAIN SIGHT OR JUST
UNDISCOVERED

I t is a distinct possibility that Nefertiti is still laying somewhere in her sarcophagus just waiting to be discovered. After all, she must have been buried somewhere, and it would have undoubtedly been with great fanfare and splendor. Perhaps, she lies in a tomb alongside her husband Akhenaten who it may be no coincidence that we also haven't found?

There is also the possibility that Nefertiti does indeed lie behind a secret wall in Tutankhamen's burial chamber, moved there when he returned to Thebes. This, however, may never be discovered as the latest position from the Egyptian authorities still lies with the fact there is nothing there.

A further position we need to consider is that we may have already found Nefertiti, not necessarily in the form of the '**younger lady**' or the undiscovered chamber, but maybe in plain sight. Sarcophagi and mummies have been found that are royalty and remain unidentified. Perhaps Nefertiti is indeed one of these.

Finally, we need to accept the possibility that we may never find the great queen's mummy, it may remain undiscovered for eternity. This, however, would be the greatest of shames since her burial chamber and sarcophagus could enlighten us as to who Nefertiti really was.

❧ VIII ❧
THE LEGACY OF NEFERTITI

❧❧❧

In order to understand the legacy Nefertiti left behind her we first need to evaluate what she truly achieved, and how that changed the coming future. We also need to determine if she truly was the most powerful queen and if she was the only one!

WHAT HAS NEFERTITI LEFT
BEHIND

❧

With the limited facts and evidence of Nefertiti's life available it is hard to decide what legacy she has left behind. She was clearly a powerful queen that assumed some of the duties of her husband, the king, but also one who only took the power allowed to her. There is no evidence to suggest that she stole power for herself, rather that she was guided and still a subservient wife to her king.

❧

You could also say that part of her legacy lies within her beauty. Her face now adorns a thousand face creams, and her bust is considered the epitomy of what a beautiful woman should be. However, this may also not be her true legacy as CT scans done on the Nefertiti bust in 2009 revealed that underneath the beautiful surface that we see there lies a more realistic image. This image is one of a woman with less symmetry, wrinkled cheeks and with a prominent bump on her nose.

※

So, if Nefertiti's legacy does not lie within her own strength and beauty, perhaps it lies in the religious revolution that she achieved alongside her husband, Akhenaten. This, however, was only temporary with Tutankhamen restoring the worship of Amen in his third year of rule. Amarna and the cult of Aten were abandoned, forgotten, and left to crumble.

※

It would be nice to be able to say that Nefertiti and Akhenaten left a legacy of powerful kings and queens to follow them, but this also wouldn't be true. Nefertiti, herself, gave birth to only female children and the two boys that Akhenaten did sire died young, albeit on the throne. They also left no male heirs to reign on their deaths, and the crown passed out of the family.

※

Furthermore, future pharaoh Horemheb would annihilate virtually all record of the cult of Aten and its founders Nefertiti and Akhenaten. They were even struck, along with Neferneferuaten, Smenkhkare, and Tutankhamen from the timeline of kings. Nothing Nefertiti and her husband created would survive much beyond their deaths.

OTHER QUEENS AND WOMEN OF EGYPT

❧

In order for us to be sure of the claim that Nefertiti was the most powerful queen in Egyptian history, we need to take a closer look at the other queens of the era and the role of women in general. After all, we cannot ascertain power in a field we have little knowledge of.

❧

We do know that women who lived during the 18th dynasty of ancient Egypt had a freedom that made them unique. Not only did they have the same legal rights as men, were allowed to own property, and work outside the home, but they were also allowed to live alone and raise children without the protection of a male.

❧

This didn't, however, raise them to the same status as male as few women received a formal education and nor could many read or write. They also were not given the opportunity to train for careers, and rather they were expected to marry and produce children. Mothers did, however, command great respect within the home and their community.

Given this information, it is clear to see that women in ancient Egypt were not the second-class citizens we may have expected to find which leads us to the conclusion that queens of Egypt were perhaps also not so much the second fiddle to their husband.

Looking at queens prior to Nefertiti we can see immediate evidence that they may have been considered more equal to their husbands than her particular story would have us believe. Tiy, Nefertiti's mother-in-law, is a particularly good example of this very idea.

Like his son would do after him, Amenhotep III took an unknown bride named Tiy to be his queen and made it very clear to everyone that she was not just a minor wife or concubine, but that she was his consort and queen of a great empire. Almost immediately Tiy lived up to his assertions and quickly became a force to be reckoned with. A powerful and influential queen with a huge public profile was born.

It needs to be stated that Tiy was not the first strong queen to rule alongside her husband. She was, however, the first to step out from the shadows of her place behind the king and into the light of being an important political figure. Tiy, like Nefertiti after her, was regularly depicted beside the king, almost as his equal.

We could, therefore, assert that Nefertiti, rather than being the forefront leader of subsequent strong and powerful queens, was actually shown the way by Tiy. This, of course, does not make light of the power Nefertiti clearly had but it does show that our train of thought she was the first is clearly wrong.

The natural argument to make now would be that Tiy never went on to rule over Egypt whereas Nefertiti potentially did. Surely this makes her, assuming the Nefertiti as king theory is correct, the most powerful queen of Egypt. This too, however, is not true. Egypt had been ruled by females before Nefertiti and would be again after her death.

There are potentially six women rulers of Egypt, but only four have been confirmed. Nefertiti and a 1st dynasty queen named Merneith are the ones that cannot be verified. Sobekneferu, Hapshetsup, Twosret, and Cleopatra VII Philopator are the ones that can.

Though little is known about the first confirmed queen to have ruled Egypt, evidence has been discovered to confirm it. Sobekneferu ruled in the last reign of the 12th dynasty taking over from her brother Amenemhat IV after he died.

❧

Also prior to Nefertiti's potential reign as king of Egypt was Hapshepsut who took power seven years into her reign as queen. As a symbol of her new kingship, she ordered that all representations of her include all the regalia and symbols of being Pharaoh. During her reign, she went on to expand trade and create a myriad of ambitious building projects. Her reign lasted over twenty years and is considered by scholars to have been one of the most successful in Egyptian history.

❧

Twosret is another confirmed ruler of Egypt during the 19th dynasty. However, like Sobekneferu many dynasties before her, little is known about her time as a king. She took the throne on the death of her son and heir officially declaring herself pharaoh. It is unclear whether her reign was ending by death or civil war.

❧

The final queen of Egypt has to be at least as famous if not more than Nefertiti herself. We have, however, far more information about her and her reign. Cleopatra married her brother Ptolemy XIII at the request of her father's will but made it very clear, very quickly that she would be the one to rule, not him. She fell from power around 48BC, but as we know, that was not the end of her fascinating story. She would go on to ally herself with Julius Caesar and reclaim her throne.

It is clear from the information above that Nefertiti was not the groundbreaking powerful woman we think of her as. Rather she was simply a successor of, or predecessor of, other equally powerful women. This does not, however, take away any of the achievements that she made in her life as queen of Egypt. It simply makes them, perhaps, not as extraordinary as we thought.

❧ IX ❦
AFTERWORD

❦

It is incredibly difficult to create a true portrait of a woman who has so little documented fact recorded about her. There are no words written down that she ever spoke, and no actions portrayed that did not stem from her husband. She is a true mystery of the ancient Egyptian world.

❦

This hasn't, however, stopped us from trying to piece together her life and bring some sort of picture of Nefertiti as an individual to life. How successful we have been in this I don't think we will ever know. So little about the woman herself has been discovered that none of us can claim to know her.

❦

What we can say is that Nefertiti has become for the modern world a symbol of female empowerment in a time that we believe males ruled. This, however, perhaps is only a figment of our imagination. The records show that Nefertiti was not the only women to assume some power in ancient Egypt and that she more than certainly didn't take it by force. As Joyce Tyldesley, a leading author on Nefertiti says,

> 'just because she (Nefertiti) is Egypt's most powerful queen in our world does not mean she was Egypt's famous and powerful queen in hers!'

In the end, regardless of fact and speculation, Nefertiti will always be known as the most famous, powerful, and beautiful of all Egyptian queens. Her very name omits intrigue, female power, and beauty, a combination which is hard to resist. No doubt, part of Nefertiti's charm to us lies in that we know so little about her and that doesn't look set to change. Nefertiti is, as unreachable to us now as she has always been, and there is no imminent sign of that changing!

❧ X ❧

FURTHER READING

✦

- The Search For Nefertiti. Joann Fletcher
- The Rise And Fall Of Ancient Egypt. Toby Wilkinson
- Nefertiti: Egypt's Sun Queen. Joyce Tyldesley

YOUR FREE EBOOK!

As a way of saying thank you for reading our book, we're offering you a free copy of the below eBook.

Happy Reading!

Made in the USA
Coppell, TX
24 September 2021